MW00948421

Find Wonder in the Ordinary.

A Kid's Book for Adults.

Right On.

Ramblings & Doodles by

Bernie Freytag

No part of this publication may be reproduced, stored in a retrieval system, or transmitted in any form or by any means—electronic, photocopying, recording, or otherwise—without prior written permission, except in the case of brief excerpts in critical reviews and articles. For permission requests, contact the author at bernie@findwonderintheordinary.Com.

All rights reserved.

Copyright © 2023 bernie freytag

Isbn: 9781072707684

The author disclaims responsibility for adverse effects or consequences from the misapplication or injudicious use of the information contained in this book. Mention of resources and associations does not imply an endorsement.

REVIEWS

In February of 2020, Find Wonder in the Ordinary won two gold medals in the Feathered Quill Book Awards. Here's a snippet from the award review:

"Adults will agree that life is an adventure of all sorts. All colors are captured: from the black and gray of sadness and pain; to the brilliant slivers of gold that come with successes; to the warm colors that always go hand-in-hand with family, love, and the ability to enjoy life to its fullest. This book is a journey that, quite literally, has all those colors. A journey of one man that proves to every reader how important the old saying, 'Take the time to stop and smell the roses,' really is."

Full review: featheredquill.com/find-wonder-in-the-ordinary

"The Stephen King quote, 'Books are uniquely portable magic', is the perfect description for Mr. Freytag's new book. Mixed in with deeply personal stories, he takes you on a funny, heart-warming, and thoughtful trip from Sunrise to Sunset. His illustrations are superb and fun, linking one thought to the next, one chapter to the next. If you feel like you need more time to appreciate the little things, this book encourages you to keep moving, observing, and especially to remember the things that give you joy."

David, NY

"It's the kind of book you pick up when you need a moment of calm. Or inspiration. Or nostalgia. Or if you just want to smile. You can open it to any chapter and read a bit, no need to plow through beginning to end, although that's exactly what I did because it does what any good book does - makes you want to turn the page to see what's next. It really did remind me of all the best parts of my childhood, and I know I'll be turning to it for years to come for a bit of sage childhood wisdom. For adults, of course. :-)"

Penelope, CA

"I've been anxious about where my life is headed and what the future holds and worried that I'm going to make a small mistake that will turn me on the wrong path doing a job I don't want to do, but reading Finding Wonder in the Ordinary just oddly enough calmed the f*ck out of me. Thank you."

Porter, NY (18 years old)

"A fantastic journey through the mind of the author. With his telling of stories, anecdotes and lighthearted musings we are transported back to a simpler time. This book completely captures the old saying to stop and smell the roses. There is no doubt that reading this book will help anyone realize that it's important to stop and take time for self care as we all live our lives with that daily grind. 5 stars, and I hope to see more from this author in the future."

Joseph, FL

"This book is insightful, honest and funny. The author muses over childhood memories, life experiences and observations that have shaped his life and outlook on this crazy world. Ultimately his writings and thoughts are a sort of compass that lead us back to what we once knew as children but often forget as adults...keep it simple and find Wonder in the Ordinary!"

Scott, ME

"This book brings your inner child out to play. It reminds you to actively seek out joy in the things most people forget to notice. Being reminded that we all live ordinary/extraordinary lives is a real gift. Any book that makes you laugh out loud and tear up is worth a good read. This one fits the bill."

Barbara, NY

To that wide-eyed, curious and joyful child
who lives deep within all of us.

Not the one who could be a little asshole,
the other one.

" Things just don't appear
so 'black and white' anymore."

grey Matters

*"Here's to new chapters...and learning how to
prepare for that last one."*

Unknown
(overheard in a dingy bar someplace in Wyoming)

———

There once was a young man who thought he was invincible. We shall call him Harry. Now, Harry didn't really believe he was *completely* invincible, but he certainly didn't think he could get hurt. He believed he had the reaction time and the physical ability to avoid dangerous situations. It's possible he thought he was some sort of superhero who could defy death or, at least, any sort of pain or injury. He was a silly person of about 30 years of age and didn't have a clue. He suffered from some sort of delusional confidence, if there is such a thing. Harry wasn't a reckless person, but his "confidence" did make him careless. Which made him unlucky. Which made him fall off his bicycle one day and hit his head pretty freakin' hard. Unfortunately, for Harry, he wasn't wearing a helmet.

Harry hit his head while biking around the Charles River in Boston. His bike riding was part of his training to complete his first marathon. He loved to bike in this area as he could avoid traffic, but most likely he annoyed the crap out of people walking or running in the same area as he rarely slowed down, zooming past them while enjoying the wind in his hair (remember, no helmet + Harry on a bike = dumb ass).

When he fell, he suffered a fractured skull, a severe laceration, a few broken digits...and one busted tooth. He also was knocked out cold after suffering a full on seizure. Harry was a mess.

Harry woke up in a hospital a couple days later, his family and friends all around him. He had a great family and very caring friends. He was diagnosed with minor head trauma and was ultimately going to be okay. Though this was the case, because of the swelling in his brain he would have to go through a rehabilitation that would take close to a year. He had to relearn the basics of reading and writing, as well as learning some new social skills. He would never completely heal, but he would come really, really close. His long term side-effects from the accident aren't even worth mentioning, but he would struggle with some of these very minor issues his whole Life. They were daily reminders, a gift that keeps on giving. But there was one thing that happened that he didn't expect, and believe it or not, it eventually led him to be grateful for the accident.

During the healing process, Harry would have flashbacks of his childhood, vividly reliving some Memories as if they were yesterday. Almost like a time machine. Some of these moments were pleasant, some not so much. At times, he would call his parents to confirm the stories. As his brain healed, it would rebuild those Memories. It was like reliving the past. And what really stuck with him were the days of fascination of his surroundings, mostly of being outdoors. Where he used to catch frogs at a nearby pond. Where he would wander around the woods in search of salamanders or unique rocks. He remembered playing freeze-tag on a hot summer evening, or trying to catch Fireflies in a jar. Oh, and skipping rocks, yes, how he loved to skip rocks. Sure, some of the bad Memories would creep in there, but ultimately the good Memories won the battle. The happy childhood Memories would stay with him forever. The core Memories of his youth resurfaced and reminded him that Life can be good.

Now for the big surprise. Ok, maybe it's not a very big surprise. Most likely it's pretty obvious. That was me in the story. I know, shocking, right? But, yes, I was Harry. "Head-Trauma Harry" (don't worry, I don't really call myself that). You probably figured that out by now, but changing the perspective and viewing my story from the outside, helps me understand what happened. It also entertains me a bit to view it as a sort of movie, and honestly, that's how it resides in my head. It could be a way to distance myself from it, but let's not get technical. This is not that type of book.

As the years passed, I re-learned a lot about the fundamentals of growing up as well. How to care. How to share. How to be forgiving. To have patience. How to interact with others. And how to grow as a person. Not that I didn't know these things beforehand, but relearning so much about your youth directly affects everything about the foundation of your Life. Am I a better person since then? I'd say yes, that I am. Am I perfect? Not a chance. I learn something new every day. Either about myself or about someone (or something) else. Yup, a work in progress.

During the process of recovery, there was one Memory that surfaced that stood out more than most. It was my earliest memory of being an artist. I was 6 years old, in the family station wagon, traveling to Florida...and eventually Disney World. These were the days where no one questioned riding in the "way back" of the station wagon, and that's exactly where my sister and I were. We were traveling from New York State so we had a fair amount of time to entertain ourselves. Throughout the trip, I would draw Disney characters in a sketch pad to amuse myself, without really knowing that my sister was paying close attention. Her compliments were what I remember most and I can't say that I ever really focused on that praise until much later in life. It is not just my earliest Memory of being an artist, but also my earliest Memory of being 100% elated with happiness. The joy of drawing, creating, was born at that moment. Not sure why my brain traveled back to that specific time, but bringing back that Memory truly showed me the power of the brain! Something I've learned is as essential in your Life, as the Sun is to our solar system. At times, when the wonders of the world hit me just right, I am that 6 year old boy again.

Before we proceed, please note, I have no idea if other head trauma folks experienced the same results I have. And I do not recommend hitting yourself in the head really fucking hard to achieve the path to your inner child. Hopefully, this book is a bit of a short cut to that kid. It's not a map. It's not a compass. More like a trusty sidekick who will sit next to you and help you get to your destination. Like Tonto is to the Lone Ranger. Or Robin to Batman. Or Ed McMahon to Johnny Carson. Which makes me think it's more like a drinking buddy. Either way, I think you get the idea. At times this book will feel like you are on drugs. Or I'm on drugs. Which is appropriate in my opinion, because I think most people take drugs to achieve that feeling when they were a kid. To laugh without hesitation. To grow without judgment. To dance like no one's watching. To move away from being a grown up and simply let go.

Throughout this book, I try to not get on a soap box to explain what you should or shouldn't do. No one wants that. I'm simply here to remind us all (myself included) of the simple wonders of the world. Of the Universe. Of Life. Our planet is in the absolute perfect position in the Universe to have Life. If the planet shifted on its axis even the slightest, Life would not be possible. I try not to think about that too much, because it hurts my little brain a bit, but when I do, it makes me realize there has to be a reason we're here, and we should wonder in that fact alone.

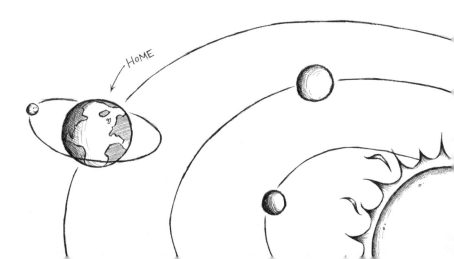

Sunrise

"It's never a bad day to have a good day."

John Sammon
(a close friend)

————

There's a little song bird sitting in a tree in your backyard, anxiously awaiting the first light of morning. She's just hanging out, without much of a care in the world, other than waiting for the damn Sun. She tweets just a little before the Sun appears, knowing we will all be witnessing something incredible. As the sky brightens, she tweets just a little more as her neighbors hear her and join in. Just a few at first, then a few more. As the rays of the Sun dance off the Earth's atmosphere, twilight has arrived and it's a full on tweeting party with all the birds in the neighborhood filling the morning air with beautiful sing-songy Music. Yup, it's a funky morning part-eee! And this is the type of scene happening just about every morning, everywhere, in every backyard, around the world. It's a celebration that we all participate in, in some way, throughout our planet. And it all revolves around a big ball of gas, at the center of everything.

Yes, everyone is affected by the Sun. Some of us may wake to it as we are enjoying our morning coffee in preparation for a hard day's work. Some may have gone out for a morning run, or walk the Dog, as the light starts to appear in the sky. Some have even put up dark blinds to ensure a later start to their day. And Animals of all kinds wander around to gather up a little morning meal. Everyone, literally everything, is affected by the "rising" of the Sun.

It takes one year for us to travel around the Sun, right? Obviously, our "Spaceship" is earth. We are rotating on our axis as we do this, and we complete that rotation every day. While we are moving in orbit around the Sun at a very slow, methodical pace, we are presented with the illusion that the Sun is rising, but we are the ones who are moving, not the Sun. You will probably say to yourself, "Well no shit, Sherlock, I knew that." But, are you reminded of this every day? I know that I'm not, as other things get in the way. I forget it quite often. The other thing that I rarely think about is that our "Spaceship" isn't really moving slowly either. Our planet is rotating at about 1000 miles an hour (this is based on the equator, and it moves slower in other parts but still moves pretty stinking fast). Also, the speed the globe moves around the Sun is about 67,000 miles an hour. Given these facts, it's difficult to understand how it could possibly create the illusion of the Sun "rising" and "setting." Yes, the Sun doesn't do anything but exist, though how it affects everything else *while* it exists, that's the amazing shit. I love the sentiment for someone's birthday to "Enjoy another year of traveling around the sun." It's possible I say it way too often, but it's a great reminder. We are the ones who are always traveling. Always moving.

As previously mentioned, the Sun is literally at the center of everything. Yes, it's at the center of our universe, but along with that, it affects everything on our planet in some way. The Sun is the purpose of all Life. It literally controls it all. It is the one thing that holds our solar system together. Think about that one for a second. It's holding us together. As it's doing this, it provides us with the necessary heat and Energy that we need for existence. Not just for survival, but existence. It truly begs for our attention. Not like a bratty kid in grade school, but more like an Oscar-winning dramatic actor, after all, the Sun *is* a Star (ahhh, see what I did there?).

If you believe in the Big Bang Theory, not the TV show, but the actual theory...you may know that during this "bang", pieces of the Sun were literally spread throughout our solar system. It was spread throughout everything it created and within all the folks who occupied our planet—slugs, bugs, birds, trees, everything. And these little pieces of Sun were passed down from generation to generation in some magical way. If you believe this, then you will know that you are also made up of parts of the Sun. In my opinion, these pieces could be what make up parts of our soul (and maybe some other cultures felt the same as their word for Sun is Sol). Yeah, no scientific facts here whatsoever, but all that aside, I do believe the

Sun is part of all of us, once again, proving it is the center of everything.

Throughout my recovery, other Memories popped up that seemed relevant. One, in particular, is about my favorite pillowcase when I was very young. Yes, I had a favorite pillowcase. It must have been important to me, as I don't remember another pillowcase before, or since, that seemed so important. This pillowcase featured Snoopy, or it could have been Charlie Brown or even Linus–tough to say as these Memories aren't always perfectly vivid. Anyway, it said something like, "How come I don't like to go to bed at night and hate waking up in the morning?" I've tried to find this pillowcase online and, at times, I've thought that maybe it doesn't really exist. But, no, I'm positive of its existence. The specifics are just a little fuzzy. Anyway, the point of mentioning it is that my Life over the years has shifted from that pillowcase to "how come I like to go to bed at night and love to get up in the morning?" Not nearly as funny, and Mr. Schultz probably wouldn't have made a dime with that saying, but nonetheless, it is true. I used to be a night Owl and refused to go to bed and then at times I'd sleep until noon on the weekends. At some point, everything shifted, and I blame it mostly on the Sun. Ok, it may have something to do with owning a Dog, but the Dog getting me up still probably has a lot to do with the Sun. Yes, I do "rise and fall", with the Sun. I like to be awake before the Sun appears and have no problem winding things down once it has gone away.

There are probably a million more reasons why the Sun is so incredible, and you probably are going through those in your head as I ramble about a freaking pillowcase, but there's a bigger message from these ramblings–how these elements affect you and what wonder you find in each. I live in an area of the country that simply doesn't get a lot of Sun. Kind of a strange thing for a guy who just babbled about the topic, and this may contribute to my fascination and appreciation for it. Don't get me wrong, we do get our share of sunshine, but on average we probably get more Clouds. We have more grey days throughout the year than we have sunny ones. But, the Sun could not ask for a better partner in crime than Clouds, who simply don't get the respect they deserve.

"Honey, could you pull over?
I think I have to sprinkle."

CLOUDS

"When you're a kid, you lay in the grass and watch the clouds going over, and you literally don't have a thought in your mind. It's purely meditation, and we lose that."

Dick Van Dyke

———

In a remote part of the desert, a cute little Cloud appeared out of nowhere like some sort of strange wizardry or ancient magic. Just moments earlier the sky was totally clear, with no Clouds and a blazing Sun. Where this little cloud came from is only known by the powers that be. Smarter people who understand such wizardry would say it had something to do with a temperature that reached well above 100 degrees, so I guess, something had to give. Our puffy friend started to grow at a rapid pace and was quickly joined by many other Clouds. They all got closer and closer and together created a huge gathering in the sky. As they grew larger, they also grew darker. The Clouds developed into a full on rainstorm, with thunder, lighting, the whole shebang. The rain that fell into the canyon was rejected by the solid ground and hard rock surfaces. A flash flood ensued and put on a show of its own creating temporary waterfalls and rushing chocolate rivers reminiscent of Mr. Wonka's wonderful factory. All of this was created by a cute little Cloud that materialized out of freakin' nowhere.

Clouds get a bad rap. People tend to dislike Clouds as they bring rain and they cover up our beloved Sun. Clouds are essential. Clouds are functional. Clouds are underrated. Clouds are beautiful.

Clouds make any photograph look better. Scratch that. The partnership of Sun and Clouds makes any photo look better. Not just photos either, but also in the real world, every day. It is that inclusion of Clouds that is essential. Any Sunset or Sunrise aficionado will tell you that. The

Clouds create depth throughout the sky, and it's always been my experience that the partnership between Sun and Clouds is the best possible combination. Just the right Balance.

Not too long ago, I had the honor to go to Ireland and re-trace some of my ancestry. Toward the end of the trip, I went for a very long walk upon the shoreline of Galway. It was a beautiful day that was not only accompanied with a sky balanced with the perfect Clouds and Sun, but also deep conversation with one of my closest friends. We were solving all of life's biggest questions, of course, and after our walk, I asked if we could just sit in a certain spot in the grass before catching some lunch. As we laid in that spot in the harbor for all of about 10 minutes, I watched the clouds slowly form animals in the sky, mor-phing from one animal to the next. One would look like a dinosaur. Another like a hippo. One small cloud broke from the pack and slowly dissipated into thin air. This is one of Life's greatest free activities. I was going to say this is one of my favorite "pastimes" but I'm not a huge fan of that word. I know the definition of the word is to pass time in a pleasurable way. But, for me, it's not about passing time. It's more about Time standing still for a second or two. Or at least slowing down. And that 10 minutes of looking at the sky at that moment seemed more like an hour. I'm sure Stephen Hawking would have a lot to say about that, but I do believe, if you are in the right frame of mind, you can slow down Time. Or, maybe Mr. Hawking would rather call that stretching Time... oops, maybe it's Dr. Hawking. Sorry, dude. Anyway, I did promise not to get on a stinkin' soap box, so, moving forward...

Every once in a while, I have the honor to fly on a plane. I'd honestly hold my arms up in the air the entire flight if I could. It's one of the coolest experiences ever, in my opinion, and it isn't just about the fact that you are traveling at several 100 miles an hour, or reaching ridiculous altitude within our atmosphere. For me, it's mostly about the clouds. Of course, everything looks amazing from that level, but I'm not sure it would be quite as beautiful without at least a few clouds. How they sometimes blanket the earth, looking so cozy I could envision myself taking a nice little nap upon them. Or how you sometimes travel right through the Clouds and appear in a different landscape on the other side. Obviously, when the Sun is involved, the appearance becomes a whole new ball game. I'm sure there's a study out there that shows why this combination can appear so "heavenly" or "angelic", but my assumption is that we tend to include religion when the beauty hits a certain height (pun somewhat intended). There could be a desire within us to see something that brings us closer to "God". It could be instilled in us to refer to Clouds as the heavens so we've been conditioned with angels already in mind, and let's be honest, it probably does bring you closer to your God. Even if you aren't that religious, the feeling of being closer to a higher power is there. Your God is simply more attainable in this particular situation, and anything that achieves that is certainly worth taking the Time to look.

Clouds part. Clouds move together. Clouds dissipate. They vanish. They appear. They evolve, morph or break apart. Nothing is forever with Clouds. They never stay still and are always moving. Changing.

"Must be spring,
saw my first human today."

CHange

"We are no longer the knights who say Ni! We are now the knights who say ekki-ekki-ekki-pitang-zoom-boing-z'nourrwringmm."

Graham Chapman

Native Americans believe you must be in tune with the changing world around us in order to live a healthy, happy, and harmonious Life. Their beliefs and lifestyles are both fascinating and enlightening. For some reason, I've always had a strong connection with their culture, so much so that I even told people in college that I had Native American blood in my heritage. I'm a little embarrassed to admit this, as I do truly respect their beliefs, but I think I can blame most of my fake facade on tequila. Which also made me tell people I was a prodigy pugilist at a younger age, which was probably my excuse at the time for having a rather wide nose. Crazy the things we do at a younger age. Well, at an older age too, as I recently had my DNA test done and was still secretly hoping for some Native American in my blood. But alas, I'm a mutt of many other breeds which I do embrace, though, I will always wonder at the Native American ways, especially their connection to just about everything. Which brings me back to the reason I brought this up in the first place—how they view Change and how they relate the Life cycle to the seasons. To them, each seasonal Change is magical and is celebrated extensively.

Spring represents Birth—a rejuvenation of Life when the smells of nature awake and fill the air. The trees start to bud as the birds appear and celebrate with song. After a long Winter, we all feel like singing "Zippity-freakin-doo-da" while skipping through a meadow, as a bird lands on your shoulder (ok, I may have dated myself with that reference, but you probably get the idea either way). This could possibly be my favorite season.

Wait, nope, Summer is my favorite. Summer represents

Youth. As it arrives, we see the Sun reaching higher in the sky. The days grow longer. The mornings appear earlier. The evenings seem to last forever. You enjoy driving with the top down and try to perfect your cannonballs into the lake (or pond, if that's your thing). This tends to be most people's favorite time of year, coincidentally similar to how many of us view Youth as our favorite part of Life. Eventually Fall creeps in and slowly Summer becomes a distant Memory. It's such a hard transition at that time of year, but Fall is when things get serious!

Fall represents Adulthood and to me is the epitome of Change. As the plants adjust their lives and prepare for rest, we are greeted with colorful shifts in the landscape. This is the true season to explore. The bugs disappear, the colors are amazing and the beer tastes so good after a long hike in the brisk air. There is nothing quite like Fall. Yes, this is my favorite. No doubt (seriously, I'm not kidding).

As the year moves forward we are greeted by Winter, which represents the Elder. Definitely NOT my favorite season, but I do enjoy it. When Old Man Winter has arrived, it's time for the appreciation of a beautiful snowy landscape. Who wouldn't love to snowshoe through the woods or have your Dog enjoy the snow like they've never seen anything quite like it (and maybe they haven't)? For me, Winter is a time of productivity, reflection and personal growth (coincidentally, it's when most of this book was created). Please allow me to quote the literary icon, Phil Connors of "Groundhog Day" fame, "Yet we know that winter is just another step in the cycle of Life. But standing here among the people of Punxsutawney and basking in the warmth of their hearths and hearts, I couldn't imagine a better fate than a long and lustrous winter." Ok, maybe that's stretching things a bit, but it is a cozy time of year still, filled with magic, and I dig that. Interestingly, when it's Winter, most people look forward to Summer. Not unlike how a lot of us, as we get older, look fondly back to those younger days of our Youth (pretty trippy, right?).

I'm lucky to live in an area where we have four true seasons. It doesn't just get cooler in the Winter, we get snow, and lots of it. This is the type of Change that I truly enjoy. Sure, when it's Summer, I can't think of anything better. Then Fall starts to creep in, the nights get a little cooler and the days a little shorter. It's then that I start to get that feeling that the time for Change is ok. This feeling is common at the start of each season. We are saddened by the passing of one season but celebrate the start of the new one. Just like starting a new chapter. There is a harmony to the Changes within nature, and the seasons show this to be quite true.

Albert Einstein once said that "the measure of intelligence is the ability to Change." I don't know if I have any business relating my thoughts to his, but here it goes. What I believe Mr. Einstein is trying to convey is to be open to all possibilities. So, it's not necessarily a physical Change, but to allow your thoughts, your curiosity, to flourish. From what I understand, this was the foundation of all of his work. He also said that he wasn't necessarily smarter than others, but he spent more time solving problems. Obviously, he was pretty humble, but by his example, he showed the power of our minds, and how that power isn't truly unleashed without the ability to Change.

The world would be a pretty boring place if it wasn't for Change. The seasons are a great example, but even within our seasons there is Change. The Fireflies only come out for a fraction of the Summer. Certain plants don't bloom until late Fall. The Winter doesn't get serious about itself until there's a deep freeze. The Changes are inevitable and once we accept their pattern, their cycle, it's then that we are truly enlightened. As the Native Americans may have felt, I also feel that Change is where Faith may live.

"Please, teach me the prophecy of the fence
of which we cannot see."

Faith

"Every time I hear that phone, it's ringing."

Unkown
(overheard at the Village Tavern, Clinton, NY)

———

After my accident I wanted to travel more, see more, feel more—almost like someone knocked some Life into me after recovery. I felt that I had not seen enough of the world, or of our own nation for that matter (and I still feel that way at times). I had an idea to drive across the country with no real plan other than to head West. A friend joined me in the journey. At the time, I lived in Boston, and it would take us several days to get to our destination. It was a lot of driving, but we were determined to see as much of the nation as we could. The fact that we did this trip less than a month after 9/11 could probably make for an entirely separate book, but to say the very least, it definitely set the stage. Towards the end of our trip, we ventured to the North Rim of the Grand Canyon. We arrived at the campground at night, secured a spot and went to sleep without really seeing the canyon because of the time of our arrival. We planned to get up early and hike around part of the rim to a lookout point. The morning arrived, and I grew antsy during the hike and asked if it was ok to pick up the pace and separate from my friend. He was fine with that as he wanted to take his time. Something pulled at me to hurry. I got to the lookout area way ahead of my friend, and I was the only person on that ridge at that time. The canyon was completely covered in fog. You couldn't see a thing. I felt a little confused and bummed as I thought I wouldn't see a thing. I sat on a rock and waited for my friend to arrive. Within minutes at the ridge of the canyon, the fog started to lift. It slowly revealed a canyon filled with fog and light that created shadows and patterns like nothing I'd ever seen before. After many days on the road, frantically trying to see as much as possible within a two week period, at this moment, I had found peace. I'd never been touched by such beauty in my Life. Looking out over the vastness of the canyon, I had never felt so small, yet I didn't feel alone. Tears poured down my cheeks. If I didn't feel the urge to hurry, I would not have had that moment of wonder. Something in the air drew me there to arrive right at that moment. Something I couldn't see, but I certainly felt. I had found my Faith.

I don't see this chapter being about religion. It's not about finding God or salvation. Not that there's anything wrong with that (Seinfeld reference, circa 1993). At times, I wish I had the dedication and commitment to be a part of an organized religion, but I think I'm part of an unorganized religion, that is occasionally organized. That may not make any sense, but for some reason it makes perfect sense to me. Being a spiritual person, you find Faith in your surroundings, in the elements of the earth and stars. Faith in nature. It's a belief that everything is somehow connected and there are times when everything can simply align and be perfect. And with a belief of this nature (pun definitely intended), there is no doubt that a higher power is evident. And it's not about finding Faith in one power either, it's about finding Faith in all things, as I also find Faith in creativity, Music, Dogs, Animals, the Sun, fire, time travel, good food, lucid dreams, belly laughs, etc. The list goes on and on.

Oddly enough, I work a desk job. I've worked in an office setting for close to 30 years. At times, my job is outside but they are very random and fleeting moments. I do have a window at the office that helps me, but ultimately, I'd rather be outside. It's where I feel the most relaxed, the most at peace. Since I work in such a place, and since I live in an area where at times you shouldn't be outside (our Winters can be quite cold and unfavorable), I find I have to cram in time with my Faith. Whether it's a walk in the woods, a run in the park or just to sit on a deck near a lake, or...go someplace in my mind (more about that later), it is at these times where I understand Life more. I've joked that when I've gone on a kayaking trip to a remote lake, or climbed a remote trail on a mountain that I'm going to church, and that's the truth. I would love to work less and spend more time at church. Who wouldn't? But that's simply not the real Life. I have to put in my time at the office, get a paycheck and make ends meet. In many ways, we need that Balance of what we have to do, with what we want to do. Inside that Balance, there is peace.

"Well, first I'm hot...then I'm cold...
then I'm hot, again..."

BaLaNCe

*"Happiness is when what you think, what you say,
and what you do are in harmony."*

Mahatma Gandi

———

Here's a little something about the day I turned
50 years of age. It isn't so much about turning 50
as it is about serendipity. The reason I mention the
exact age is I think that has something to do with the
story, since it's a milestone age and all. All that aside,
it's a pretty simple story about how the Universe goes
through an interesting little dance at times.

That morning I went to a yoga class well before the Sun came up. Seemed like an appropriate thing to do to start the day. After the class, we were greeted by a Sunrise that set the sky on fire with a magnificent colorful display. I mention this only because without that Sunrise, I'm not sure how grounded I would have become as it really made me pay attention to all elements throughout the day. Eventually, I was driving to work and listening to the Tom Petty station on SiriusXM radio. Yes, I'm obsessed with Mr. Petty, and was lucky enough to see him perform several times throughout his career. An amazing human. If you don't know, his station isn't just him playing his music, but a lot of his inspirations and sometimes other artists are featured covering his songs. On this particular occasion, they were playing Tom's song "Honey Bee", but it was performed by Widespread Panic. While this was playing all I could think of was how I never really got into Widespread Panic, but always liked one particular song. But for the Life of me, I could not remember what that one song was called. It totally escaped me at that moment. The day went on, and I quickly forgot about those thoughts. It ended up being a very long day, filled with many little wonderful moments, as well as a lot of love from friends and family. Toward the end of the evening, I was driving home, and I turned the station over to the JamOn channel and...dun, dun, dun... yup, over 12 hours later, at that precise moment, the song I was trying to think of by WSP was playing. I'm fairly certain that I haven't heard that song in at least 10 years, but there it was. And where this really hits home is that the title of the song is "Ain't Life Grand". And yes, at that moment, that's exactly what I thought, too. Ain't. Life. Grand. A song oddly enough about the pleaure found in basic, simple every-day activities.

Now, turning a "milestone age" is a pretty silly thing and as I've always said, it's only a number. But when the Universe reminds you through subtle hints and clues, it justifies the journey. Stories like this one happen to me way more often than you could possibly imagine. At some times, they totally freak me out. But at other times, like this one, it reminds of the wonderful Balance in the Universe, and that just puts a smile on my face.

Balance is all around us and this is probably not any truer than in the Balance of Nature. Obviously, we know the

Sun provides Energy for our planet. Plants flourish for exactly this reason. Herbivores eat the plants. Omnivores eat the plants as well, but they also eat the herbivores that eat the plants (starting to sound like a Dr. Seuss book). Plants take in carbon dioxide from the air and release oxygen. Animals breathe in air and release carbon dioxide. Plants and Animals depend on each other. Birds and bees depend on each other. Nature relies on Balance. We rely on Balance. Our emotions depend on each other, our work and play depend on each other (there's got to be a song in there somewhere).

Ever have a moment where you recognize a Balance within your own Life? Could be as simple as you just lost something of minimal value and then you find some money in a pair of pants you hadn't worn in a while. Most likely these things happen when you weren't really paying much attention and are suddenly surprised. Obviously, not everything in Life is perfect, but sometimes it does equal out when we are not paying attention. It's possible that it could be related to the Secrets of the Universe that we simply don't understand. At times, I witness these examples of Balance throughout the day. Sometimes several times in a day. Sometimes I don't see them at all.

But when I do, it's always subtle, and noticeable only when I'm not really paying attention.

I was raised a Roman Catholic and still embody a lot of those teachings (minus a lot of the guilt of course, although that still rears its head at times). One of my favorite messages that I still adhere to each day is one of the 10 Commandments: "Do unto others as you would have them do unto you." Another message is that "God only gives us what we can handle," which I believe someone shortened or summarized from a passage in the Bible. A less religious statement, but a statement that is always rustling around in my brain, is, "That which does not kill us, makes us stronger," written by the German philosopher, Friedrich Nietzsche (my hat off to that dude). Quotes like these are important in our Life. It's a great way to give credit to many people before us. I have various quotes that I keep at the back of my brain, only to bring them out at random times. A lot of them are Music lyrics, which at times can be Biblical to me (more about that later). The one thing the quotes in this paragraph have in common is that they all represent some sort of Balance (obviously, that's the name of the chapter so it was a pretty good clue). "Doing unto others" is basically saying whatever you put out into the Universe is what you will get back. Nietzsche's quote tells us through tough times, we gain wisdom or strength. It's a Balance of give and take. Dark and light.

In my opinion, Animals may be the most fascinating part of Balance. In fact, they are probably the most fascinating part of Faith and Change, too. Ok, they are the most amazing part of most things, period. It's possible that I learn more from the behavior of Animals than I learn from the behavior of humans. This can go back as far as I can remember and is probably why I've always had an Animal at my side through most of my Life. Yeah, my Dog. I'm not sure who I'd be if I didn't have a Dog, but I'm pretty sure my Balance would be off.

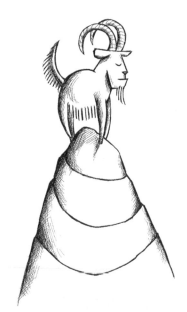

"My love isn't as unconditional
as you people think."

Dogs

"Be the person your Dog thinks you are."

J.W. Stephens

———

Once upon a time, there was a Dog who was in love with the Sun. On summer days, where the Sun was obviously more abundant, you could find him panting on the back porch until you'd think it would become unbearable, yet he stayed right there. When inside, you could always find him where the Sun appeared through the window and onto the floor or couch. Always in the Sun. If it was a partly Cloudy day and the Sun went behind the Clouds, he would go find his human and just stare at him. On occasion, he would even bark, demanding the Sun to reappear. He was a riot.

This Dog was my boy, Floyd, and it's possible he didn't really even know what the Sun was. He just wanted to be warm. He had a heavy Orvis sweater he would wear in the winter months and always wanted to sleep under the blankets, even in the summer. When it was time to wash this favorite sweater of his, he would sit next to the washer/dryer until it came back out. He was a quirky Dog with an abundance of personality.

Unfortunately, at the age of 6, Floyd was diagnosed with bone cancer in one of his legs. The leg needed to be removed so that the cancer wouldn't spread quickly. They said if his leg was not removed, he would live for about 3 months. If the leg was removed, he would live about 6 months. If the leg was removed and he went through chemotherapy, he would live for about a year. Opting for the most aggressive path, miraculously, Floyd lived for almost 2 more years. And in that time, simply by example, he taught me more about Life than any other human.

Obviously, I was hesitant on his leg removal, but through a lot of research, it made it clear this was the way to go. Dogs' minds are so different than ours that he simply wouldn't miss the leg and he'd adapt quickly. Someone even wrote online that, "Dogs are born with 3 legs and a spare." It was something I didn't really believe at the time, but Floyd would prove this to be very true.

The doctor said Floyd would need to spend two days with them after the leg removal to recover. After just one day, the doctor called and said Floyd was ready to go home. He was restless and moving around without any issue. He said for me to keep him from exerting too much Energy for about two weeks which proved to be the hardest task as Floyd just wanted to go. There was no recovery time for him. There was no time for him to learn to use three legs. He simply did it. It slowed him down considerably of course, but he was immediately ready to live.

I probably have a 100 stories of Floyd's amazing spirit. It's difficult to discuss at times as I do feel he didn't get enough of a chance to truly live. He passed away just shy of his 8th birthday. Not long enough, in my opinion (56 in human years if you don't care to do the math). But, for the time he was here, he certainly filled his days with determination and joy. I remember being reluctant to take him on a hike in his later years, but when I did, he didn't slow down in the slightest. He reminded me to continue doing the things he loved to do. I rarely left Floyd alone in the years after his surgery, at first because I wanted to ensure a good Life for him, but after a while it was because his thirst for Life was so infectious.

Dogs live in the moment. They never think about the meaning of Life. They never contemplate their existence. They don't complain about their problems. They simply keep moving forward. Living. Being. Loving. They don't worry about what may have been or what could possibly be. And yes, they love unconditionally. They don't care if you have a zit on your forehead. They don't care if you've gained weight. They don't care if you have grey hair. But, what they do care about is Life.

I was recently told that as a child, when playing "house" with some friends, I always wanted to be the Dog. At times, I still want to be a Dog. What a Life they must

live. A Dog can truly Balance anyone's Life, and I think
without a Dog I sincerely would not know who I was.
It's possible that the Dog is my spirit Animal, too.
But, then at times, I feel like my spirit Animal could also
be a Fox, or an Owl, or a Monkey, or a Frog, or a Spider,
or a Butterfly...

Animals

*"Some people talk to animals. Not many listen, though.
That's the problem."*

A.A. Milne

In an earlier draft of my book, this was the story I was
going to have at the start of this chapter:

*I had just moved into a new house. I wasn't anywhere
close to settled in, but I was doing my best. I bought the
property primarily for the view, where I could see about
10 miles through rolling hills, as well as a clearing that
was closer to the house. The clearing was where deer
would usually gather. But on this particular day, as I
was getting ready for work, I suddenly looked out the*

bathroom window into the backyard and saw a flash of fiery orange. A rather large Fox had passed through the clearing, the first Fox I'd ever seen in the wild. And for the rest of that day, that was all I thought about. Why did the Fox run across at that particular moment? If I looked at that window a half a second later I probably wouldn't have seen it. Or even earlier, as I probably wouldn't have continued looking for very long. But for that very brief moment in time, I connected with that Animal. And he (or she) connected with me.

Around my last time reading and editing the book, I thought about changing this story. Embellishing a little by saying the Fox actually looked up at me as I looked at him. I haven't embellished on anything else within this book, but I did think that addition would make for a better story. Not unlike how some movies are "based" on true events. Sometimes, the possibility is tempting. So, I wrote up the alternate story and thought I would decide if it should be included at a later date. The very next morning, on my way to work, a Fox crossed the road in front of me. An even larger Fox. He stopped, turned to look at me, and then moved on. At the time, I thought that was a sign that I should include my fabricated story. But, obviously, now I understood that it was a suggestion to tell the absolute truth. And to further illustrate just how connected we are to Animals.

As a spirit Animal (yes, I do think we all have these), the Fox reveals itself during times of unpredictable Change. Although moving into a new house isn't unpredictable. Everything that a new house reveals is uncertain. Especially the house I bought! Built in the mid 1800s, it certainly needed a lot of TLC. I'm sure the same type of message may be true about the second time I saw a Fox, and part of me would like to think it was the same exact Fox. But, all the spiritual mumbo-jumbo aside, seeing a Fox in my own backyard and crossing the street in front of me, was just damn cool!

I've always been attracted to Animals (no, not like that, you sicko). From a very young age, I could be found drawing Animals of all types. Not really understanding why, other than I liked the way they look. Over the years, I've learned to respect Animals more and more, and I now see them in a different perspective. And when they reveal themselves, it's a special moment...and yes, they reveal themselves. As weird as that sounds, I believe they know more about how the world works than we do and will appear when necessary.

As I mentioned, most of my fascination with Animals is visual. Being an artist, I guess that's where it usually starts. But seriously, let's take our friend the Fox, for example. Not all are a fiery orange, but the most common ones are. Their sly eyes, pointy snout and ears, combined with their color and a bushy tail, make for a very unique look that you simply don't see any place else. The visual wonder of an Animal will continue to sustain me for many years to come. I simply cannot see a day when I'm not amazed over the look of a creature, tame or wild, and hope that you have also had such an experience. For me, you could mention just about any creature and I would find something fascinating about their appearance. Even though this fascination runs deep, the wonder doesn't end there. The behavior of Animals can run even deeper.

As I was writing this book, I did a little research here and there. Most of my "research" was my personal observations, but sometimes I would run across something that would just blow me away. Again, we are back with our friend, the Fox, as our example. Remember, this is some fun info about just ONE creature. Multiply that by many thousand, perhaps millions and you will never want to hear your kid say they're bored again (sorry, that's a soapbox discussion that I'll try to avoid). Anyway, through some of my readings I learned that although Foxes make for very good parents, they are surprisingly solitary and don't travel in packs. They can also be quite playful and can enjoy certain elements of nature similar to a cat who enjoys a ball of yarn or a Dog enjoys a ball. Cool stuff for sure, but wait for this. There are studies that suggest Foxes hunt for food using the earth's magnetic field to hunt. What's that? Yes, scientists are starting to believe that they can focus on mice under three feet of snow by using the earth as their guide. Honestly, I don't know that I even understand this in the slightest, but I certainly hope to witness it in action some day. For now you can Google that shit and be in awe of the videos you will find of a bounding Fox diving head first into the snow. They need complete silence, and the slightest distraction can throw off their trajectory, but when the conditions are perfect, and they are facing true north, they will catch dinner 75% of the time! With information like that, it's no wonder I think Animals know more than we think.

Suffice to say, this is the case with each and every Animal out there. There's always something to discover, always something that fascinates–something beyond the visual beauty. But, at times, the visible beauty is more than enough, too.

"But, I wanna ask the bigger questions.
Like how, and what, and especially, why!"

OWLS

"The Owl is the wisest of all birds because the more it sees, the less it talks."

African Proverb

———

There is a majestic, spiritual quality to many things in nature, but nothing more magical than the mystic ways of Owls. It's not necessarily a Harry Potter type of magic, but a real, out-of-this-world type of magic. It's a magic you cannot see, but it's surely there. I had never seen an Owl in the wild until a couple years ago, and since then I've seen just a handful more. Each time I've had an Owl sighting, they have revealed themselves in similar ways. Yes, again, like most Animals, they reveal themselves.

And it was the day I saw my first Owl, that I had that thought.

My first sighting was early spring, or maybe more like the end of winter, but either way, there were no leaves on the trees, so the woods were quite stark. My girlfriend at the time had done some research and found out that this was the time of year the Barred Owl would be out throughout the day, as it was their mating season. I guess when they feel like getting it on they don't sleep? I don't know. Anyway, we decided to see if we could find these beautiful creatures, so we gathered up our Dogs for a hike to see what we could find. We searched and we searched. Looking high and low (mostly high), but even with the barren forest at that time of year, we surmised that it may be impossible. An Owl could blend right into the surroundings. At one point, toward the end of the hike, I decided to walk ahead a bit with the Dogs. As the Dogs and I walked down the narrow trail, I was ready to give up looking, when I thought I heard a very subtle sound, almost like a whisper. Was that a "who?" No, it couldn't be. They don't really "who", do they? I kept walking. My focus had turned a little Cloudy as I felt a calmness come over me.

I simply thought these were the effects of a walk in the woods which was usually the case. As I was questioning these feelings, the most peaceful face suddenly appeared in front of me, a very sleepy looking Barred Owl, perched on a dead tree about 30 feet in the air. As peaceful and calm as could be. The Owl was at least 50-60 feet from me, but at that moment, I felt like it was right in front of my face.

As crazy as it sounds, I feel that little Owl spoke to me that day saying, "I'm right here. If you are open to it, you will see me. Let your mind go, believe that I'm here, and you will see." In retrospect, the feeling I had just before seeing him felt like a trance, almost like he was pulling me toward him. Or maybe something else was pulling me there. Since that day, I've seen a few other owls, and they all revealed themselves in similar ways. It's quite possible that they don't appear to everyone. It could be more of a feeling to see them rather than a desire. Obviously, if it wasn't for my ex-girlfriend, we never would have been there to begin with, but I sincerely believe that we never would have seen that magical creature if we didn't let go of the desire.

I can only wish that everyone will experience the majestic feeling when seeing an Owl. It's not something I can easily explain and certainly not anything I'll ever forget. Just to see how their head can swivel is a treat in itself. And yes, they certainly do say "who". Although not technically a song bird, the Barred Owl does have an amazing song of its own where it sounds like he sings, "Who cooks for you? Who cooks for you all?" And if you ever get the chance to listen to the Great Horned Owl pairing with another Owl, you have the amazing opportunity to witness one of the best natural symphonies performed in nature. I've had Great Horned Owls just behind my house for a while now, and I still have not seen them. I've heard them many, many times, but never a sighting. I guess they can be a little shy and a bit more territorial than the Barred Owl which could be there reason I haven't seen them, but I like to think that they simply have not decided to reveal themselves...yet.

~~Primates~~ MONKeys

I don't have any amazing stories about Monkeys. I don't even have a quote about Monkeys. I've never seen a Monkey outside of a zoo. All I know is that I've always loved Monkeys and marvel at their mischievous, playful, inquisitive, silly nature. I also like to say the word, Monkey. Monkey. Monkey. Apparently, I like to type it too. Anywho, for this section, I'm simply going to list all the things that I appreciate about the Monkey (mostly factual):

1. Monkeys like to climb things, but not many swing from branch to branch. Most of them walk along the branches. Now you know.

2. Monkeys throw their poo - which is really a sign of aggression and not as much fun as it may sound.

3. Some Monkeys will pee into their own hand and rub it on their fur to attract a mate. Homemade cologne.

4. The tip of a monkey's tail has similar characteristics of a fingertip with tiny ridges to help them grip better.

5. A group of Monkeys can be called a tribe, a troop or a mission. Evidently, they can also be called a carload or a barrel, if you can believe that.

6. A group of baboons can be categorized as a "congress"... which explains a lot.

7. Monkeys can understand numbers and can count, some have been known to understand multiplication.

8. Monkeys express affection with others through grooming. No wonder I marvel over them—so weird and cute at the same time.

9. A type of Monkey in China rides deer for transportation and will groom the deer as a way of saying thanks. Again, can you stand it?

10. Monkeys obviously eat bananas, but they do not eat the banana peel. Which seems like a pretty silly fact, but I guess some people are shocked by this. Who the hell eats the peels anyway?

11. Monkeys have tails, apes don't. Which I believe is an unfair reason to not consider an ape a Monkey. Unless an ape prefers to not be considered a Monkey. Than that's different. But, seriously, who wouldn't want to be Monkey? At least for a day.

12. People get mad when I refer to Monkeys as Animals. "They are Primates," they say. But aren't we all Animals? And I'm pretty sure I'm not offending anyone, am I?

13. Speaking of Primates, I think all Primates should be called Monkeys. It's a better word than Primate, and I'm fairly certain Apes won't give a crap about the name Change.

I've always been a big fan of nature documentaries and can be completely enthralled while watching them to the point where I don't hear people talking to me while watching. I've watched many of them and usually I don't retain a lot of the facts, but I do marvel at the imagery and details of the Animals. When the Monkeys are featured, it's all over. I've been known to replay these sections over and over. The way the Monkeys move, behave and communicate is fascinating. I've never really had the desire to travel to a remote country to witness these great primates and prefer to consume my observation remotely. It's not that I'm afraid to travel there or anything, but I simply prefer to allow the Monkeys to live in their natural habitat without human interference. I know a lot of the documentaries I've seen do not interfere and document from a distance, so I feel this is okay. I have been to a fair amount of zoos and am a bit torn on their purpose and necessity. Without getting onto that soapbox of mine, I do have a story of a young Orangutan in the Audubon Zoo in New Orleans.

While visiting New Orleans with friends many years ago, we decided to spend our last day riding the trolley that happened to stop at the local zoo. It's something I rarely do, but it seemed like a reputable zoo, and it would give us a much needed break from Bloody Mary's and crawfish etouffee. Most of the

Animals didn't seem thrilled to be there, which didn't help, but everything Changed when we got to the orangutan area. Their area was particularly open, and there were no fences or enclosures, just a large moat around their area that led to a high wall. There were two adult orangutans along with a smaller orangutan who I assumed was their child. There was a trainer in the area with them who had a microphone and was commenting on their habits and behaviors. It was basically a show. All of their activities were planned for some silly response from the audience, which they responded to in kind until the highlight of the show. They gave the younger orangutan a large t-shirt to play with. Thinking he was going to put on the shirt as part of the show, we were all pleasantly surprised when he wrapped the shirt around his neck and started to run around the area like mad, with the t-shirt flowing in the wind like a cape. Super orangutan was here! The audience exploded with approval! The orangutan was a total ham and was fueled by the applause and laughter. We eventually found out that the orangutan was born in captivity, hence his drive to please the audience. He simply adjusted to a lifestyle that was presented to him. He didn't know any better. I don't know if this is right or wrong, but boy did it settle into my Memory, only to be revisited occasionally, almost like it was yesterday.

Yes, I realize I said I didn't have any stories about Monkeys, and given that orangutans are technically not Monkeys, that statement is still true. But, semantics aside, what I learn from ~~Primates~~ Monkeys, is that it's okay to be silly. It's okay to be playful and a little mischievous at times. Grab a t-shirt and act like a superhero if you want to. Swing around and act like a fool if it makes you feel good. Do what makes you feel happy. Enjoy the ride.

"I call it Eat. Prey. Love."

Spiders

"Piece of cake...how hard can it be?"

Bernard Freytag Jr.
(my father speaking of just about every project he ever started)

———

An ugly little Spider is hanging precariously upon the strands of its web, basking in the Sun. Dew is hanging perfectly off the strands and creating a glimmer with the Sunlight. The web is a work of art, and our friend waits patiently upon it to snare their prey. Suddenly, a hand appears out of nowhere and wipes out the Spider's home with a swoosh as he flies off into the water below. Hardly shaken, the Spider immediately starts to head back to the boat upon which its web was being built. Not long after the desecration of its home, Mr. Spider finds his way back to another area and starts to spin another glorious web just in time for lunch.

My parents are now retired, enjoying their golden years at a lake house throughout the summer. They have a nice little party barge that they tool around in from time to time. Every morning my mother will clean the boat of Spider webs. Yes, every morning. Don't get me wrong, having Spider webs all over the boat isn't the best thing, but it just fascinates me that these Spiders are not fazed by the destruction and simply go right back to work each day and rebuild their homes. Sometimes several times in a day. And each web is a freaking masterpiece. The intricacies of each web are incredible and can be built in about an hour. Not that I've ever sat and watched this, but I certainly wouldn't mind.

People hate Spiders. They are pretty crazy looking, for sure, especially when you witness a really large one the size of your damn fist. But, I love Spiders. I love how they move and how they hunt. Not to mention that the silk that they produce is one of the strongest natural materials in the world. Which is why Peter Parker is such a damn stud! And one of my favorite super heroes...but I digress. We are here to talk about Spiders, not Spider-man. But, yes, the material that they produce is unbelievably strong, even though it seems just the opposite. And this does prove that Spiderman could really swing around town on the webbing that he creates...well, theoretically of course.

Spiders eat insects. A lot of them. Want to really get freaked out? There are approximately 30,000 species of Spiders throughout the world. What? True, Google that shit! But, seriously, most Spiders are good! They Balance out the environment and make it less buggy. Less insects. More intricate web designs. What's not to love?

If you find a Spider web outside somewhere, especially an orb-weaver, don't destroy it right away. Take note of it and go look at it again in the early morning when the Sun is about to rise. Most likely it will have dew on it (if not, wait for a day that dew has formed). I guarantee that is a moment you will not want to miss. The web will be glistening with the sunlight. If there is no Sun "out" at that time, I think you would still have a decent experience. And if you don't, then get rid of the web, pour yourself a nice cup of coffee and just enjoy the day!

There's a poem by Robert Frost called "Design", where he's speaking of how a Spider appears in nature on a flower holding a moth. I've added this poem to the end of the chapter for your reading pleasure (and because it's just so damn well written). I should say, although I enjoy poetry, especially Mr. Frost's stuff, I'm no expert. I can barely tell you what certain poems are about. Hell, I barely know what this poem is about, but I do have an inkling of an idea. This poem has really stayed with me over the years, and the reason I share it here is that the message of that poem is perfect to close out this chapter. What has stayed with me over time is the overall meaning of something so small having a "design" to it. The question of how could it be so well orchestrated, and do all things in nature have a "design" to them? It's why I find wonder in most things, and it fascinates me that a Spider can produce something so perfect. So amazing. Over and over, without hesitation or thought. I applaud you, Mr. Spider. Your work is inspiring and shows us something to strive for. Now, get back to work!

Design

I found a dimpled Spider, fat and white,
On a white heal-all, holding up a moth
Like a white piece of rigid satin cloth--
Assorted characters of Death and blight
Mixed ready to begin the morning right,
Like the ingredients of a witches' broth--
A snow-drop Spider, a flower like a froth,
And dead wings carried like a paper kite.

What had that flower to do with being white,
The wayside blue and innocent heal-all?
What brought the kindred Spider to that height,
Then steered the white moth thither in the night?
What but design of darkness to appall?--
If design govern in a thing so small.

Robert Frost

"Well, she changed a little more
than I expected."

Butterflies

"Your ancestors call it magic, but you call it science.
I come from a land where they are one and the same."

Thor

Imagine for a second, that you have about 14 legs and you travel slowly through Life, eating leaves and trying your best to avoid being stepped on. Not the best Life, but things do get better. Your main purpose in Life is to make it to a branch or something, attach yourself to it and then start the process of metamorphosis, where you spend a short period of time in a cocoon, where you do God knows what, and emerge as a freakin' Butterfly. Being proud of yourself, you gather up all your brothers and sisters for a day or two of frolicking around, testing your wings and then simply fly off to greater horizons. If you are lucky, you will take a not-so-straight flight to Mexico where you will meet up with many other handsome devils, just like yourself, and possibly a sister or two. Hopefully not ending the trip on the windshield of a semi or nabbed by some parasitic fly. If you defy all odds, you could live this amazing Life for about a year. Sounds pretty cool, doesn't it? For any amount of time, yes, I believe it does!

The length of a Butterfly's Life aside, how freaking amazing is their story? They start out as one thing, they lock themselves into some sort of caterpillar-made coffin and perform one of the most amazing magic tricks of all time. Forget about science fiction tales. This is some real Life craziness. Correction, it isn't like magic, it IS magic. It's like seeing a triple rainbow! That shit just doesn't make sense.

All of that aside, have you ever really looked at the patterns on a Butterfly's wings? It's like when they are in their pupa state, they're painting elaborate patterns on themselves. That's quality time with one's self right there. And they say that no two Butterflies are alike either. I'm not sure who is out there comparing, but I guess that does make sense.

Years ago, I lived outside Boston and worked in Harvard Square. Near my office on the Harvard campus is a small museum that I stumbled upon one day when I had visitors in town and we were looking for something to do. It's the Harvard Museum of Natural History if you ever want to venture out that way and check it out. Anyway, the museum is filled with many cool exhibits, but to me, nothing compares to their collection of Butterflies. If you ever want to sit in a room and wonder over the many amazing colors that Butterflies have created, this is the place. Then go grab a chicken pot pie and a pint at John Harvard Pub and Brewery (well worth it).

Nature is filled with magical moments and Butterflies are a prime example of just one. Like how a chameleon can Change the color of their damn skin to blend into their surroundings. How ants can work tirelessly in unity like a bunch of marching soldiers and lift at least 50 times their own body weight. How a beaver can cut down trees and build his home with his goddamn teeth, for Christ's sake. And these animals do all of this without any concern for what we think, or how they look. Their one single purpose is survival. To adapt and live. And most of them live a much shorter life than we do. It's almost like they are born with the answers on how to truly live and have less to learn.

"Honey? Does my butt look big
in this light?"

Fireflies

*"In order for the light to shine so brightly,
the darkness must be present."*

Sir Francis Bacon

———

It was a hot summer night—the kind of night where once the Sun set, you were still a little warm with just a t-shirt and shorts on. A group of us had gathered at a friend's apartment, nestled in the woods in rural Vermont. We were having a great time, telling stories, laughing. The moon was bright, the stars were brighter. You could not have asked for a better night. The apartment was in a barn that sat on a hill with a path behind it that led into the woods. Once the Sun had completely set, our host invited us to go on a moonlight walk into the woods. She spoke of a pond that the path would lead us to. The opening to the wooded area was pitch black. We had to put complete Faith in our guide as she led the way.

As we entered the woods, we eventually had to hold each others' hands as we couldn't see a thing. How cute is that image? A bunch of 20-30 year olds holding hands and giggling through the woods. So adorable and silly! Anyway, at the time, I wasn't sure why we didn't have a flashlight or headlamp to guide the way, but this was way better anyway. If you looked up, you could make out the dense outline of treetops. Clusters of stars filled the sliver of sky that was visible. I had my head facing skyward the entire time we were walking as the stars were so visible, I couldn't take my eyes off them. As we kept walking, the treetops widened and the stars multiplied. My focus started to shift down from the sky, and I caught a glimpse of a flickering star that seemed to move, then another, and another. It was then I realized, as we arrived at the pond, that the area was filled with Fireflies. I had a hard time telling where the stars ended and the Fireflies began. My mouth opened wide as I collapsed to the ground. I was in complete and total awe to what I was witnessing. Speechless.

I've always had a fascination with Fireflies. Seriously, who wouldn't? Their damn butts light up! And who wouldn't want to try and catch them in a jar and save them as their own? And as with Butterflies, the Firefly also lives a very short Life. They basically live from mating season to mating season which usually starts around May or June, depending on where you live. And it's during this mating season we get their epic shows. For the most part, they flash their butts to attract a mate which is usually the primary reason most Animals do just about anything it seems—to get some action and pass along their heritage and their bloodline. It is their instinct. It is their blood whispering to them. "Go get some, you wonderful little firebug!"

Their gathering is a total "single's scene." All these lightning bugs get together and flash their butts to impress other lightning bugs, flirting and showing off their best self. "Hey, look at me! Hey, how you doin'?". Very similar to how a party would work for us human folks just that we wear fancy clothes, get our hair all stylized, and put on silly fragrances instead of flashing our butts at each other. They just put on a show, they attract a mate who digs it, they fool around and have some babies. Pretty simple really.

The simplest of motives and the simplest of actions can truly be a beautiful thing. It's an inspiring display to witness. And to know that there is a lot more going on in a Firefly display than merely a fancy light show is pretty damn cool! As with other displays similar to these actions, they are fleeting moments that only last for a very short period of time, a fraction of the Summer months. Not only are these displays something to look forward to, they are something to completely cherish while they are here, as they won't be here for long. You can relate that however you wish throughout your Life, but I simply like to look forward to when I'll see those beautiful light shows again.

Take in every second of them when they are here.

Then you can relive those lasting Memories,

over and over, in your mind.

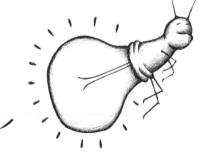

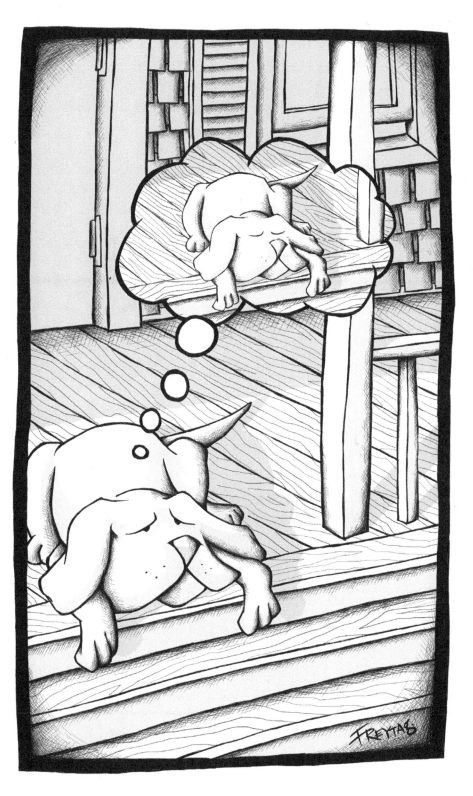

daydreaMing

"I was trying to daydream, but my mind kept wandering"

Steven Wright

———

In the middle of the afternoon, I go out West, traveling through the mountains of Colorado into the dry heat of Utah, meandering through switchbacks that hug the rocky landscape along the muddy waters of the Colorado river. Quickly, I jump to the mountain biking trails of Moab. Just as quickly, I leap over to the slot canyons of Zion. The burger at Oscars outside of Zion is cooked to absolute perfection and is washed down nicely with a cold local brew. As I travel through these Memories, I'm very much aware that I'm not actually out West, but at the office, ready to get back to whatever the hell it was that I was working on.

I think we all have our own ways of meditating that probably fall outside of the traditional sense. Some of us take bubble baths. Some of us enjoy a glass of wine, or any type of "me time". Some put headphones on and listen to Music. Some even zone out to Cloud formations in the sky. And some of us, like me, Daydream. It's a perfectly legitimate practice that I believe should be taught in schools (and I happen to know a few teachers who would agree with that statement). The impact of Daydreaming can be paramount to any lifestyle. If you have the time, simply let your thoughts drift away, and explore the power of your brain.

In a kayak, on a remote lake in the Adirondack mountains, we are surrounded by colorful leaves and a brisk Autumn air. The occasional leaf falls and lands softly on the water, creating the illusion of little boats. The Sun is warm, but the air is cool and invigorating. The water is like glass and the kayak cuts through it cleanly, with little sound.

Staring at a screen for 8 hours a day is counter-productive. There I said it! And there is no way you should work 100% of the time that you are at work. Obviously, there is a Balance and you still need to get the work done, but it's very productive to allow your mind some of its own time. There are times when I can't figure out something, it makes sense to go for a walk or drive. When that's not possible, I can go for a little journey in my mind, and sometimes, if I'm lucky, a solution is presented to me. There are a lot of employers out there who probably would disagree with this statement, but screw them. How the hell would they ever know? Sometimes good, old-fashioned hard work is the answer, but, I firmly believe that pressing pause can sometimes be the way to move forward. Let the mind wander, and you will find your way.

Oh, to be a Musician, and spend the days on the road, traveling from town to town. A guitar is my only companion. Wait, is that a song lyric? Anyway, oh, the idea of playing every honky-tonk joint and seedy bar from Nashville to Telluride. Could I bring my Dog with me? Yeah, she can come with me. But then the guitar is not my only companion. Oh well, maybe I could write my own song

about how my dog and I play Music throughout the coun-
try. If only I could quit it all and travel the Music circuit.
Hmmm, probably should be better at singing...and gui-
tar...and songwriting...and...

These examples are only to show that anything is fair
game with Daydreaming. Could be about a past trip.
Could be about a future trip. Could be about a job you'd
rather have. Maybe a person you'd like to meet. Or a
person you'd like to *be*. And it could be totally unrealis-
tic, too. And it doesn't necessarily need to be unspoken,
either.

On our cross-country trip so many years ago, we eventually made our way to Yellowstone, and obviously had to
stop at Old Faithful which I believe should now be called
"Old and not so Faithful" as it doesn't erupt as timely
anymore. But all that aside, as we were waiting for the
show, a young family with three young boys were sitting
nearby. It wasn't the busiest time of year so we could hear
their conversation perfectly. One of the kids asked what
was going to happen when Old Faithful actually erupted,
and the younger kid, possibly the jokester of the family,

started to come up with outrageous answers–everything from Starburst candy to tapioca pudding. Then the oldest son added in that a whole bunch of prairie dogs are going to shoot out! Everyone started to crack up. One of them asked if they had wings, as the other added they would be playing banjos. This gave me an image of a fat little cherub-like prairie dog that always stayed in my head (and just happens to be the sketch at the end of this chapter). The joy that these children brought to this situation was like nothing I've witnessed in years, and it's always a reminder to me that silly is good. Stretching the possibilities in your mind doesn't have to be based in reality. Have fun with it and your thoughts can bring you any place imaginable.

Daydreaming thoughts that are brought into reality is not more evident than with art, especially books and music, as I believe they really are the best tools to allow your imagination to explore. Which brings me to a great example by Tom Petty (yes, again). He wrote a song called "It's Good to be King". This tune talks playfully about what it would be like to be the king of your own town and how it not only woud help to make friends, but to also meet girls. Where he's allowing our mind to take us to a place where it's ok to be free of any outside influence, including logic and reasoning. A way to escape and let the mind wander. Songwriters are some of the best Daydreamers around. There are probably a million songs out there about just that. Another favorite of mine has to be Lyle Lovett's "If I Had a Boat". Where he ponders what it would be like to have a boat to take out to sea, and if he had a pony, he could ride it on his boat. So illogical, yet creative and beautiful in its absurdity. It's this kind of thinking that brings us right back to that mindset of a child where there are no boundaries of logic or fact. Music can be one of the ultimate playgrounds for creative thinking and expressive thought. And it's possible that it's one of my biggest obsessions.

"It was just a matter of time
before one of us went electric."

MUSIC

"Give this song a listen to feel like you're rocking in a hammock, in the summer, looking at the stars when the Sun is just starting to go down. Also, you are barefoot. That is all!"

Micaela Honsinger
(my niece)

It's late in the evening as I'm laying in bed. I'm probably all of about 4 years old, and I'm listening to my parents and their friends enjoy a night of music and laughter. This was a common situation as a child where my father would entertain friends while playing guitar and singing songs by artists like Paul Simon and Jim Croce. I'm not really sure how good he was, but I do remember finding comfort in the distant sounds of people singing along to some classic tunes. Okay, they were mostly laughing as they all tried to sing along, while consuming adult beverages. Amazingly, these sounds would eventually rock me to sleep (pun intended...again), and to this day, not only does the Music of Paul Simon and Jim Croce bring me right back to those Memories, it's also been common in my adult years to perform an Irish exit and go to bed while a party is going on, just to listen to that comforting sound of a party in the distance.

After my accident, I latched onto Music, both live and recorded, like never before. I lived in Boston so I had accessibility to Music every day of the week if I wanted. And at times, I would take full advantage of that access. I would also go back and rediscover albums from my youth that brought me great comfort, similar to Simon and Croce, though these were songs from later periods of my Life. Bands like The Police and U2, that filled my teenage years. Or INXS, REM and the Fixx. Man, how I loved the Fixx! The Police happened to be my very first concert way back in 1983. Not too shabby for a first concert, I must say. But, it really doesn't matter what I've listened to, and I'm not here to brag, either (ok, maybe I'm bragging about my first concert a little, but can you blame me, really?). My point here is that Music, in a lot of ways, has guided my Life. It has helped me through some of the most trying moments you could imagine. I've actually said that Music saved my Life, and I don't think that's much of an exaggeration.

There's an old saying that Music can soothe the savage beast. Actually that's a shortened version of the quote, but it works better than the original, so there's that. Anyway, what I love about that saying is that no matter what mood you're in, Music can Change that mood. Or comfort that mood. Or enhance that mood. It is possibly the most powerful of all holistic medicines, without actually being something you ingest. I'm sure there are a lot of studies out there on how Music affects your brain, but I think they would be pretty obvious. In my opinion, it is like a drug. It's addictive, habit forming, and I'm completely obsessed with it.

Music can be transcendent. It can take you on a journey without you ever taking a step. It could take you to the freakin' moon and back in one song. And who doesn't love singing along to one of your favorite songs at the top of your lungs while in the shower or in your car? You may want to know what type of Music is my favorite, but I sincerely feel that it doesn't matter, and it's a personal choice. If you like to listen to Death-polka, I wouldn't judge (I'm not even sure there is such a thing, but I'd like to hear it if there is).

Recently my niece told me that she loves the beginnings of certain songs–how the song builds at the start. Since she told me this, I started paying attention to the same feature in songs and have started to build a mix of these songs on my phone. Compiling a group of songs based on similarities can be a very therapeutic practice, and it is yet another example of finding wonder. Or maybe more specifically it's finding wonder in the simplest thing that can be connected. Making mixes is something I've been doing for a very long time, and I'm not really sure I ever thought about the connection aspect, or the wonder aspect, until my niece told me about her new obsession. Looking through my iTunes now, I have mixes based on the Sun, the Moon, breakups, long songs, short songs, killing songs, mellow songs, groovy songs, traveling tunes, singer/songwriters, duos, etc. And at other times, the Balance in Music can only be found when the songs have absolutely no connection in common at all, other than simply being great.

Some people take in the Energy of their surrounding, which is why I'm usually not a fan of crowds. Everything shifts when I'm at a live show. Everyone is there for the same purpose, so the Energy is shared. And if it's a show where everyone is singing along, or even if everyone is truly engaged, it can create an Energy that if bottled, could possibly create world peace. Yes, it is that power- ful. I've joked at times, certain shows are like a micro- cosm of how I wish the world worked. Everyone on the same page, on the same note, just there to enjoy the beau- ty of what Life can create. Everyone dancing around like planets in orbit. Or maybe it's more like the strange and mystical patterns of a starling murmuration. If you ever want to argue that this is not the case, I would tell you to look up the Queen show from Live Aid in 1985, and you will witness exactly what I'm talking about (if there were ever 20 minutes where I could be transported back in time, that may be the moment).

Bob Marley once sang the best thing about Music, is when it hits you, you don't feel pain. When Music truly hits you, it takes you by the hand and takes you on a path where you are truly free—a ride away from everything else that could possibly be bothering you at the time. Again, it is another way of feeling younger as it could bring you back to a time when you didn't have the pressures you have now. It could move you like you haven't moved in years. It can transcend you to another time, another place. To the freakin' moon and back.

THE ORiGiNAL STRiNG THEORY

Space

"The sky calls to us."

Carl Sagan

———

We sit here on a planet in the middle of a solar system that is absolutely enormous. Eight planets, all rotating in a perfect dance in the heavens (ok, 9 if you still believe in Pluto...poor, poor Pluto). To help illustrate how large this truly is, I'd like to show it in comparison to what's relevant on Earth. If you were able to drive continuously around the globe, it would take about 25,000 miles to do this (close to a month or so at an average speed). The moon is about 234,000 miles from us, which would take us about 5 months or so to drive there. Side note: it took us three days to go to the moon back in the day in a stinking Spaceship (you do the math on how fast that sucker was moving). Now, getting back to more natural things. Our closest planet is Mars and that's approximately 39,000,000 miles from Earth. And the Sun, is 93,000,000 miles away. You can easily figure out how that relates to our 25,000 miles to circumnavigate our planet, which gives you a very good understanding on what is "out there". But remember, these are just the closest planets. This doesn't even come close to the stars that are out there. And how some stars may actually have solar systems like ours. Or that some light that we see on Earth that we think is a star, is actually a collapsed star but it was so far away that the light is still getting to us. Yes, and most stars we see at night are actually light years away! Mind. Blown.

Looking out into Space on a clear evening may be one of the coolest things there is to see. Not just for the stars, but the possibility of more. If the elements are just right, you have the opportunity to see incredibly far without the help of a telescope. You could easily see

Mars and Venus without much trouble. But, you could also see Jupiter and possibly Saturn when the conditions are just right. Obviously, it's just a light in the sky that looks like a star, but it's a damn planet. And some of these planets are way larger than earth. **WAY LARGER!** Jupiter is more than 11 times the size of Earth. And the Sun is about 109 times our size!

When I think of Space, I sometimes think of a children's book by Dr. Seuss. Stay with me here, as this may get a little trippy. The book I'm thinking of is *Horton Hears a Who* where an elephant hears something coming from a piece of dust on a flower, and it turns out to be a tiny village of people. Well, they are "Who's" and this elephant just discovered "Whoville". But where it gets really heavy, is that I picture this as a metaphor for our Universe. And if you think about it, the elephant could be living on a piece of dust in someone else's "Universe". Or in Whoville there could be a piece of dust with another little village in it. The possibilities are endless as we don't really know what is truly out there, so anything is possible. To take this one step further, I also think that on this little piece of dust in this story, outside of this little town of Whoville, there is a Grinch who's plotting to ruin Christmas. Yeah, told ya it may get trippy.

Simply put, Space can both fascinate me and freak me the fuck out. To think about its size, well, we don't even know its true size really, because we don't know when it ends. But, there are possibilities out there that scare us and intrigue us at the same time. It's much the same way we view our own lives. We don't really know how any of this will play out, and at any moment it could all just disappear. Fascinating, and terrifying! But, we enjoy the beauty of it while we're here. And it reminds us of just how small we are. And just how small our problems are. There is a Balance in the Universe that I don't think we understand, and that's no more evident than in space. Animals react to the Sun and Moon and we chalk it up to instinct because we really don't know how to explain it. But, I believe it's all connected. The moon, the stars, the Animals, everything. And it's possible that the Animals may be holding onto the Secrets, and they may not even know what those Secrets are. It's just something they do, blindly and without thought. I don't know that any of this is true, or how it holds up to scientific fact, but, I guess this is where Faith enters. To believe in what we cannot see, the unknown...or not yet known. It invigorates me with the passion to explore more, to experience more, and to try and understand more about what Life has deemed its Secrets!

Secrets

"Oh, I have an idea...let's just sit and see what happens."

Joe Lopata
(a close friend)

———

On a trip to Yosemite National Park, my companion had to make a phone call in the middle of our first day. The village at the center of the park was the only location where you could use your mobile device, so that's where we ended up. I decided to walk around the village, maybe get a drink or something while I waited. Strangely enough, you can actually buy one beer in Yosemite at the market in the village. Who knew? Talk about "finding wonder"! Ha! Anyway, I bought a Sierra Nevada (seemed appropriate) and wandered outside to find a place to sit down and do some people watching.

I looked at all the benches, and they all had people sitting at them. There was only one bench to sit on, but it had another person there. Being a mildly introverted person that looked pretty full to me. But, I ended up approaching that bench anyway and saw it was an elderly man of dark complexion, holding a cane and talking on his phone. I didn't want to interrupt but when he saw me approach he lowered the phone and gestured, "Can I help you?"

"Anyone sitting there?" I whispered.

"You are," he claimed, and after a short pause he added, "I've been waiting for you."

At the time I didn't think much of the gravity of this statement. I simply thought it was a joke, but after our conversation, I wasn't so sure. My bench sidekick went back to talking on his phone. It sounded like he was talking to a son or daughter. I wasn't eavesdropping, just sounded like he was, and it was impossible to tune it out. After some idle small talk he ended the call and turned to me.

"Kids are wonderful. You got any children?" he asked.

"Kinda. I have a Dog." It's how I usually answered this question, and he seemed pleased with my response.

"Ahhh, so you are a caring individual. Then you understand what it's like to be responsible for another being. Good, glad we understand each other. What brings you to Yosemite?"

I went into the whole story of where I was from, why I was there. He listened intently, and I felt like he truly cared. I asked him in return where he was from and responded with quite a bit more than just that, in just a few minutes. Where he was from, about his first wife, about his career, about his children and how much they meant to him. Then he spoke of his second wife.

"I'm out here with her and a group of travelers. They hiked up to a point where you can see Yosemite Falls. As you can see, I can't really do any hiking", as he lifted his cane, "Yeah, just left me here on this bench...that was 4 years ago!"

I reacted quickly to this statement, almost giving myself whiplash, as I looked at him wide-eyed. He was looking off into the distance, slowly turned to me and said, "Gotcha!"

"Oh man, I was going to say. Ha! That's hilarious. I need to use that some day," I bellowed.

"You're welcome to it. I definitely borrowed that from someone else, I'm sure," he said.

He asked more about kids and family and I think he could tell that I wasn't giving anything up in that category. He probably started to pick up on something when he finally asked, "Do you know what the Secret to Life is?"

At this point I was so engulfed in the conversation, I almost didn't answer.

"Oh, I have some ideas on the subject, but I'd love to hear your 'Secret'," I remarked.

"Well, the Secret to Life is very simple. It's actually one

word. And we already touched on it earlier in our conversation." He paused slightly, I believe for a little dramatic effect.

"It's respect," he said. "In every situation in Life, it all comes down to respect. Respect for your parents who raised you. Respect for your children to be the individuals they want to be. Respect for another's religion. Respect for someone's nationality. For their lifestyle. For the color of their skin."

He paused to look at his watch. Although there were hundreds of people nearby, it seemed like we were the only ones in the park. Everything else just faded away. Then he added, "Respect, my friend. It's not just some Aretha Franklin tune." He nodded at me again, with a wink.

He went on to tell me more about respect and how our leaders could have more respect for other countries. How any relationship needs to be based on respect. Our conversation ventured into several other topics as we waited. Most of the topics were trivial and good hearted. We eventually met up with our companions, or they met up with us. We exchanged a few words at that point and eventually parted ways.

That conversation truly Changed how I view people. It Changed how I view a lot of things, really. I could have gone anywhere in the park at that point but I decided to sit on that bench. I was meant to sit there. It was a beautiful day that I will always remember...and when I do, it grounds me. And it also reminds me of the "Secrets" others have told me.

At around the time I bought my first house, my grandfather on my mother's side was visiting and stopped by to see the new place. He used to be a bricklayer back in the day, and had a great understanding of houses and buildings in general. After I gave him the tour of the house, pointing out all of the projects I had going on, he said, "You know, that's the Secret to Life. Projects!" It's a statement I've always remembered, and I probably always have that sentiment at the back of my mind as I jump from project to project. One project can always lead to others.

For example, the cartoons you see at the beginning of each chapter grew from a project I had of trying to get a cartoon published in the New Yorker. I probably conjured up about 100 cartoons before I decided they should be part of a book instead. In fact, some of the cartoons in this book started as rejected New Yorker cartoons (it's my Secret which ones). Until now, I wasn't really sure why I was creating all of those rejections, though now I do believe they were practice for me to publish here. Life is strange that way.

My grandfather I spoke of earlier had an older brother who also kept a Secret to Life. He was just as active as my grandfather and could be seen walking around town or shoveling his own driveway well into his 90s. We eventually lost him at the ripe age of 102. His mind was just as sharp right up until his passing, and I would relate that strongly to the Secret of his longevity. When asked of this Secret, he simply replied, "Always keep Moving."

"Here's a new one. Try and keep up."

Movement

"All I know...is wet birds don't fly."

Bernard Freytag, Sr.
(my grandfather)

———

After my dog had his leg removed, he still wanted to move. Although he did tire more easily, he never became lazy. As I mentioned, his determination and passion for Life was infectious, and after his passing, he inspired me (once again) to train for a marathon. It would become my own way of honoring him. I decided to run the Mount Desert Island marathon in Maine—a tough course, but a beautiful setting hugging Acadia National Park. Obviously, knowing what I went through the last time I trained for a marathon, I had a lot to overcome. The training was my favorite part of the entire experience as I would spend hours in the hills around my hometown. Just me and my thoughts. It was during these runs, that I started to understand that doing a marathon was mostly mental. Until I actually ran the course, I'm not sure I truly understood that statement.

The day of the marathon approached and the weather, for lack of a better term, was crap. Approximately 40° at the start with a slow drizzle, and the forecast was for more rain as the day progressed. For the most part, the run went ok, but there were some trying times and unfortunately a lot of the great views were covered with Clouds that weren't the type I would find favorable. If you are not aware of the course, miles 22-25 are basically uphill. And not just a small climb. At about mile 23, the skies started to darken and the wind became angry as the temperature declined further. The rain started to come down in sheets as my spirit started to bend. I slowed considerably and started to question what I was doing. It was probably the only time in my Life that I truly turned to the heavens and questioned everything. I questioned Faith.

I questioned myself. But, I kept moving forward. At the peak of that climb, the wind slowed, the sky lightened and the Sun tried to show itself, but the Clouds still prevailed. I eventually finished the race and only had three thoughts in my head. The first, although a bit dramatic, was how grateful I was to be alive. Even though I was quite fatigued, the Energy within me was invigorating. The second thought was how grateful I was that my boy, Floyd, was there with me that day (yes, I can be pretty sappy). The truth is if it wasn't for that Dog, I probably wouldn't have ever finished that marathon. And the third thought was how I was never going to do that again! That was one of the most difficult things I've ever done, but...thoughts are weird. They can morph and shift and turn around. Just a few weeks later, I decided I wanted to do another marathon. This time, with a close friend less than a year later. I'm sure someplace within those thoughts, I also heard "Always keep Moving!"

You cannot have Music without Movement. Clouds wouldn't create thunderstorms without Movement. Spiders wouldn't have webs. Butterflies and Fireflies wouldn't, well, fly. The Earth wouldn't orbit the Sun. Which means no Sunrises, no Sunsets. And if you've laughed at anything in this book, that's Movement, too (one of my favorite kinds). Being silly can free you from everything that's around you, letting your mind move freely without true direction. Letting it wander is as important as letting your body do the same–something I learned on all of those training runs. Which makes me think that our physical Movement and our Movement within our thoughts are definitely connected. And possibly, just possibly, they are also related to the Movement of the Universe. Yes, everything is Moving, all the time, whether we see it or not.

My grandfather on my father's side was also obsessed with Movement. He was a postal worker most of his life–a mailman. He walked his route every day. He enjoyed his job through all types of weather and after retirement, he kept on walking. He walked almost every day to church for daily mass. When he came over for dinner, he would always want to go for a walk after. He loved to work in his garden throughout the summer as well. He simply enjoyed

Moving, and he never did it quickly. No rush whatsoever. He didn't quite live to 102, but he did reach 90 which ain't too shabby either. Not only do I share his obsession with Moving, I also share his name, and that's pretty damn cool (ok, I may also share his sentimentality and his taste for beer, too)!

As with most things in this book, my obsession with Movement goes back to my childhood. I was always an active child mostly because of my thirst for the outdoors. My mother may have thought that it was simply a desire to get dirty, but I do believe that was merely a side effect. Anyway, my parents redirected my active nature into sports which I'm very grateful for as I was somewhat of a shy kid. I gradually became a decent athlete, and I'm still pretty active. Almost every day I enjoy some sort of physical activity. I've said in passing that if I don't work out, I'm not really sure who I am, and there's a lot of truth to that. Anyway, as a kid, there was nothing like wandering around the woods and gathering up this or that. Or sledding down a hill near our house. Building a fort or taking my Big Wheel down the street to hit the breaks and spin around like a lunatic. Playing kickball on a Summer day or jumping into a lake! Ahhh, jumping in a lake! Something I still love to do to this day!

Movement isn't just about feeling good physically. It also can invigorate your brain. It's precisely why I try to squeeze in some sort of Movement in the morning. It sets my brain up for the day. And on a larger scale, traveling can invigorate the brain in other ways. I'm sure a lot of us, at times, just need to get away, and I believe that can be a desire to massage those brain muscles. It helps us to look at the World differently and ultimately, it should remind us just how powerful our brain can be.

As I mentioned before, I view the brain as our Sun. In my opinion, it has more power than any other part of our body. And when it's agitated, massaged, or at times rested, it can do the impossible. It can do a lot more than we may ever know. It can creep up on you at any time and truly fascinate you with the depth of its capacity. It can trick us. It can protect us. It can entertain us. And it can remind us of moments long forgotten. To me, this isn't more evident than when the brain is triggered to remind us of a Memory deeply rooted in ourselves. I believe this is one of the main things that separate humans from others. Not only that our brain can make this connection, but that we can recognize it as it happens and we can travel to a certain Memory without actually going anywhere.

Weeeee!!

"Just sayin', who in a million years would ever know if you made me a little thinner?"

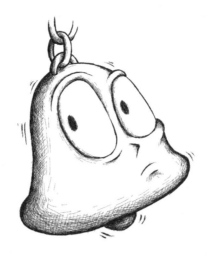

MeMorieS

"Don't worry, if I ever lose my memory, I'll try and remember you."

Rachel Cornacchia Freytag
(my mother)

———

Just after a beautiful hike, my excitement was heightened as I approached a small lake with a rocky shoreline. Yes, the lake was serene and breathtaking as it sat at the base of many mountains, but that shoreline, full of small rocks, was what intrigued me the most. Seeing that the lake was calm with no interruption and acting like a mirror, added to my excitement. No wind. No wake. Just a sheet of glass with many small rocks for the taking. I started to look through the rocks, choosing a handful of flatter ones that seemed appropriate. The flatter, the better. There's one. There's another. The possibilities were endless as I started skipping rocks upon the surface, waiting just long enough between tosses for the water to calm so that the next throw was equally effective. Some rocks traveled just a short distance, but some seemed to go on forever. Some floated weightlessly between skips as others plummeted quickly after the initial toss. This activity was medicinal as it brought with it a feeling of contentment, a feeling of comfort. Okay, it was the feeling of pure joy. This was an activity that lived deep in my childhood Memories, and obviously, those are just damn precious.

Although I consider myself somewhat of a minimalist (key word is "somewhat"), I do hold onto some items that remind me of special Memories. Yes, mementos. And if you think of it, you probably do as well, whether it's the photos on your walls or the trinkets rumbling around in your junk drawer. For me, there are a handful of things that I like to "collect" to remind me of something important. Most obvious are concert tickets, concert posters or t-shirts. These are scattered throughout my belongings.

When I see them, they bring me right back to that moment like a damn time machine.

Recently, I traveled out west for an amazing journey through Utah. As part of the trip, we rented mountain bikes and tooled around the red rocks of Moab. As we were securing our bikes prior to the ride, I noticed some lip balm for sale at the counter and knew that I needed some with SPF protection as it was damn hot at that time of year. Long story short, I carried that lip balm with me every day after. And every day I pulled it out of my pocket, it reminded me of that trip to Utah. More specifically, of the great mountain biking. Unfortunately, as with many things, the lip balm didn't last and eventually ran out. I was at the gym when this happened, and I threw it in the trash. On my ride home, I felt like I had completely lost the connection to that Memory. Pretty silly thought, but I did make that immediate connection. (Or is it a dis-connection?) Don't you worry, I decided to try and trick myself and found the same brand of lip balm on Amazon, and it was delivered to my doorstep. All is right in the world. I have no doubt that this plan will not be as effective as the real thing, but you can't blame me for trying to trick Mr. Brain. Okay, enough of lip treatment.

On a similar note, whenever I travel, I do tend to pick up something along the way that will bring me back to that moment. It can be as simple as a box of matches with a restaurant's logo on it. Those are the best as they are so simple and can be thrown in a drawer only to be re-discovered one day far in the future just to trigger that Memory. Most are concert tickets, but there are also some other things that were either passed down from my grandparents or were given to me at special times. I don't sit and gasp over these mementos like a psychopath, but it is nice to occasionally look through the Memories, similar to looking through an old photo album.

As I've mentioned, I've had a few dogs over the years and their Memories are some of the most important. One thing I've always held onto over time have been their collars and their tags. It's impossible for me to forget these beautiful beings (Cognac, Patches, Hugo, Boss, Sargent, Doogie, Floyd), but securing something physical from them is my way to remind me that they live on in my Memories. Not unlike how the Mexican culture believes this to be the case with photos of their family or friends who have passed. If you have seen the animated movie, Coco, you will understand what that means. If you haven't, it's pretty simple and possibly one of the most enduring ideas I've ever heard. You may have heard of the Day of the Dead, which is a holiday that this culture celebrates for all who have passed. On this day, the people who have passed are cherished through the display of photos. It's their belief that if the photo is not displayed, the person is forgotten and does not live on in the afterlife. A bit extreme, but I love the idea of it and have since displayed more photos throughout my home of loved ones who have passed. Not really for the fear that these people would be forgotten, but more for the constant reminder of the person's character and of all they have taught me over the years.

There's obviously some very scientific patterns that your brain follows to achieve these Memories, but I'd rather just chalk it up as some sort of magic, some sort of mystical way that can't truly be explained, to know just how precious and priceless some of these moments are and that they basically just live on in your head. No place else. And how they can be re-lived through a simple action or moment, like how discovering a rocky shoreline on the edge of a pristine lake can bring such amazing feelings to the surface. Only to be revisited occasionally when needed. Just like making Time for old friends.

"Not sure how much easier this is,
but then again, how the hell would I know?"

"Oh, yes, take your Time...all we have is Time."

Waiter
(Hamilton Inn, Hamilton, NY)

—————

After I had my accident, Time seemed to slow down. It obviously was perception based on my recovery, but it definitely felt like it was somehow being stretched. Everything appeared differently. Those who looked upon me probably didn't notice a huge difference, but my view looking outward showed a very different world. Throughout my recovery, it was common for me to see a neurologist, not just because I hit my head really freakin' hard, but because I had a seizure at the scene of the accident. Since there were no witnesses, it was unclear if the seizure caused the accident or if the accident caused the seizure. Kind of a bummer of a mystery really, as I was poked and prodded in the brain for a while to see if I could be prone to those seizures. I also had to take a medication to ensure it wouldn't happen again. Good Times, good Times. Anyway, having a routine blood test was part of those checkups and during one of the results it showed my white blood cell count was really high. Long story short, I was eventually diagnosed with a rare form of Leukemia. Literally, adding insult to injury. I had pretty much just recovered from this accident and now I was faced with a Life threatening illness. Seriously? What. The. Fuck.

When all of this went down, to put it bluntly, it scared the living shit out of me. More than the accident did. It was like a one-two punch, and the second punch was a sucker punch. And this happened immediately after my experience of reliving my childhood Memories, so it really scared me to know that all of those Memories I made over the years could be it. I may not get more happy Memories. As if the bike accident wasn't enough, at this point I was truly faced with my Time on this earth. My mortality.

In retrospect, I believe if I didn't have that bike accident, they may have never have found the Leukemia at the Time they did. Which was really, really early in the grand scheme of things. Coincidentally, a new medication was just being introduced to the market, and it would prove to be a genuine miracle drug. If it wasn't for this medication I would've had a blood transfusion and months of recovery, and that didn't even guarantee a cure. Not the best plan, but before this medication, that was the deal! At the Time of diagnosis, they basically monitored my cell count and said there was nothing to do until it reached a certain level. Throughout this period, my mind would go to really dark places, and rightly so. This wasn't some common cold. There was something growing inside me that, statistically, doesn't end well. My perception of Time, post accident, had ended and it was somehow speeding up.

The period from diagnosis to taking the medication, in retrospect, feels non-existent. I think my mind was so preoccupied with my own fear that I buried that Time away.

But, after recalling the dates of the diagnosis for writing this chapter, it all came back to me. It was the summer of 2001, the summer I was planning my (aforementioned) cross-country trip. On Sept. 26th of that year, my white blood cell count jumped to 52,000. It was Time to take the medication. Oddly enough, this was also the Time just after 9/11, so you could imagine how my view of the world had shifted, indefinitely, both on a personal and a global perspective. And my cross-country trip was scheduled to begin in early October, so that moment in Time had an incredible effect on my Life. So much so, that I could probably write another book on those few weeks alone. But, let's save that, well...for another Time.

Based on how that period of my Life made me feel, it's probably a bit anticlimactic to now say that the medication immediately put me into remission, and it's where I've been ever since. Looking back on it now, it's really how it played out. Overall, I haven't suffered much physically. The medication had some minor side effects, but nothing compared to the alternative. I only mention it now as the suffering was mostly mental and compressed my need to understand more about Life AND Death.

There is always a possibility that I'm not completely "out of the woods" and that probability is what keeps me humble. The drug did its job and has allowed me to live a happy, healthy Life. But, I'm reminded of my mortality every single day.

I have checkups every few months to check on my cell count. This keeps my Time on this planet at top of mind. In some ways, I welcome the reminder. That may sound strange to you, but I believe that with reminders of your immortality, that's when your Life truly is enjoyed. We often overlook the beauty of everyday experiences. We are prone to missing all the little beautiful things that Life has to offer. And I will say that most of the Time, my life has slowed back down to that pleasurable pace post accident.

Life isn't all roses, rainbows and unicorns. Especially unicorns, because, well, you know...anyway...Life can be really hard. And Death is probably harder, right? Especially for the people left behind. I've had my share of loss, but probably a lot less than most. I lost my grandparents over the years, and I miss them all very much.

Most of the rest of my family is still kicking and most of my friends are as well. I have lost some Dogs over the years that have really taught me a lot as they are like my children. And no one should ever have to lose a child. I don't have all the answers to Life or Death, but a lot of what I do know can be summed up in a few words really. All of these souls we've lost, are still with us. There are reminders of their existence throughout our lives, but we have to be open to seeing them. I'm not saying that they are going to appear like ghosts and sit at the end of your bed at night, though, their spirit could appear. Their Energy is with us. Whether in a situation or within someone else, they will revisit. My current Dog grew up with Floyd and quite often, Floyd shows himself in her. My grandfather can appear within my father at Times. I have a dear friend who lost her mother recently, but her mother lives in her, in her children. All of these people do live on in our Memories, and we can visit with them whenever we want. We carry them with us.

I know all of this is really heavy and there are a lot funnier parts of this book, but I'm sharing it because it's helped me. It's helped me use my Time more efficiently. To take advantage of Time. It's helped me enjoy my Time. To not waste Time. I wouldn't say that I've reached complete and total enlightenment with these thoughts, but I do believe a heightened awareness allows all of us to understand our surroundings better. And don't get me wrong, I'm not walking around like Jesus Christ or something. I struggle with these things every day. It's a part of being human. When I do remember where I've been, and not worry too much about where I'm going, it's then that Time is more precious, and it slows right down again. That's when I know to savor each small moment of the day so that Life isn't as hard, whether it's to enjoy the simple pleasure of a landscape, or to bask in a Firefly party in a private gathering in the woods. Or maybe you are into something else, like going for long walks every morning with your Dog. Or playing cards with your buddies. Or maybe it's just a good book and a cup of earl grey. The smaller moments will win overall.

I'm not sure where Life will lead me from here, and I think that's the point, really. To wander through life without holding on too tightly or not holding on enough. Every day is different and we have a choice to either coast through these moments without a care, or we have a chance to reach out and touch the pieces we want. Not everything is perfect, but I would say that certain things within ordinary moments can be. Just like how a Spider builds their web. Or how Clouds can subtly fill the sky and redirect the light without fully obstructing the Sun. How the perfect Music can transform you into a different mood, or suddenly transform you into a different "place". How the perfect dinner, filled with laughter and joy of great friends, can fill your heart. Or how the Sun, as it sets, can light up the sky with a color you didn't even know existed. Life is full of these moments that will Balance out the rest. It's within these moments that we truly feel alive.

The Sunset became even more beautiful once she understood the depth of its shadows.
FREYTAG

Sunset

"People hear ya when you're laughing.
No one hears ya when you're crying."

Taxi Driver
(on my ride from the airport to Dublin)

———

As our planet Moves gracefully around the Sun, its
rotation creates the illusion of a setting Sun. Combine
that with the Sun's orbit, and we understand that this
illusion is actually occurring continuously around the
world. Every second of every day. And it's continuously
Changing, too. The Sunset you enjoyed will be different
from the one someone further west is enjoying moments
later. The light will be different. The shadows will be
different. The "illusion" is unique for everyone. Though
somehow they connect us. I'm sure you would agree that

many moments in our lives have been heightened simply because of the "perfect" Sunset. Moments where the Sun set softly between two mountains, or was mirrored magically on a pristine lake, or how it may have created the most magnificent long shadows that seemed to last forever. I searched through my Memories to recall that Sunset that would close out this book. I searched through my travels, as well as the moments that literally happened in my backyard. I looked through all of my photos as I have thousands and thousands that have benefited from the Sunset. My conclusion in my search? There just isn't one Sunset that stands out over the rest. Each Sunset is unique. Every day is unique. There's always something unique to look forward to in each and every day.

We celebrate the setting of the Sun way more than we celebrate anything else that the damn Sun does. Sure, the Sunrise is always something to cherish and embrace, but the Sunset is truly celebrated. Could have something to do with the completion of the day. Could have something to do with the anticipation of something fun to do after dark. Or it could simply have to do with the consumption of adult beverages. I'm sure there's some really smart person out there who could shed more light on the subject (yup, totally intended). For me, the Sunset is simply about the Energy it creates. Not the physical Energy, but the feeling. The aura. Yes, it does have a lot to do with how it looks, but that's just part of the Energy as well, and that Energy is possibly what connects us all. I'm not talking about the Energy that fuels your house or warms your hot tub. It's the overall Energy we simply cannot see which I believe to be the most fascinating element in all "ordinary" things.

Every chapter in this book, in some way, is connected to Energy. Every little wonder we have. That feeling when we watch a rainstorm develop. That feeling of rediscovering a lost Memory. Or revisiting something in a Daydream. That feeling that somehow Time has slowed down, just for you. And it's important, at least to me, to remember how to harness the Energy that makes us happy. Either to seek it out, or wander around until it finds us. And it helps overall to remember those really small wonders the most. The ones that are rooted in every day. Like Cloud formations and beautiful lakes that mirror the sky. Or listening to a song bird as morning approaches. And they don't have to be in nature either. For example, let's say you like the sound of a specific word, like *sassafras*, or *bullocks*, or especially, *serendipity*. Or you smile each time the clock hits 11:11. Or you find comfort in the smell of lavender or you listen to the same song six times in a row just because you like the way the song starts. Or the feeling you get when laughing until you almost pee your pants. It could even be about a favorite pillowcase. That's it! You are already experiencing that Energy. It's always there.

As the Sun sets, it's also time to look back upon the day. Similar to this thought, this last chapter is a look back on the book as a whole. There are many reasons why the book was created, but I think the biggest reason is that when Life shows you something important, it's difficult to keep it to yourself. And with any art, it's about sharing. Oddly enough, the idea of this book, which I feel sat dormant in my brain for many, many years... suddenly reappeared in a Native American park out west, through what I can only describe as some sort of spiritual awakening. An Energy I can't really explain. Strange, right? But, I can't deny it. After reading that, you may question me and ask why the hell should you listen to a word I have said. The short answer is that you don't. You could put this book down and walk away, consider me a flake and move on. But, before you go, here are some of my confessions, the Secrets not discussed until after dark. Even though I've rambled on for days and days...I'm no brain surgeon or the freaking Pope. In short...

I'm simple.

I don't have a ton of money and live an average Life. I value my privacy and a roof over my head, but what I value most is the ability to look at life simply, through observation rather than research, at times experience rather than education. I don't consider myself smart, but I guess I've acquired some sort of wisdom over Time, and that's a different thing (I think). Also...

I have a small brain.

I've never had it officially measured, mind you. It feels small. I do have a nice picture of it someplace. Seriously, I do. And well, it looks small. Although it is small, it is powerful. A powerful weapon at times. And a powerful tool at other times. It needs its quiet Time and occasionally needs to be nurtured and pampered. It's cute and needs attention, like a pet. Sometimes it takes me a while to understand a situation. This is a work in progress, just like everything else that enters and exits this little pet brain of mine. I enjoy how the little brain works. At times, I think I'd be a great contestant on Jeopardy if there wasn't a Time limit. But then again, it wouldn't be Jeopardy, would it? That being said...

I'm introverted.

I'm not a complete introvert, but I am introverted. Maybe 70% of the time. After a day of interacting with people, I need some time to refuel my pet brain. To recharge. I've never been one to speak up in a classroom and would rather sit in the back and listen. Observing a conversation or situation is my way. I'd rather have a beer with a few close friends rather than attend a party. I'd rather do work on my own than sit in a meeting with others. I'm better on my own outside of meetings. Or maybe it's more accurate to say I'm better after meetings. I don't know. I think I just confused myself. Anyway...

I can be insecure.

I'm not completely insecure, but I can be at Times. Being a simple, slow-learning individual who's had a little head trauma can do that to ya. But, to me it's understandable to question things a bit. I always question the worth of something I've created. I've never been 100% satisfied in anything, and this book probably falls in that category as well. Will this book really help people? Am I adding anything of value to people's lives? Do I sound like an annoying douche bag? I'm nothing special, and I'm average in a variety of different ways. I'm probably below average in other ways. Speaking of that...

I'm short.

These confessions are only to illustrate that none of us are perfect. It's understandable how these imperfections can affect our Energy. Occasionally, we all may have to go through some shitty stuff, and that may be so we understand the Balance. It's just the way it is, I guess. But, it's up to us to confront these confessions, these imperfections, and learn from them. To pay attention. Which is why I've decided to share my experiences and to remind us (myself included), to look at the world differently. To know about, seek out, and embrace, the positive Energy.

From what I understand, we use about 8% of our brain. It is my belief, when the stimulation is just right, we have the capacity to use quite a bit more. The brain reacts to Energy with its own Energy. An important reminder is that the brain is nothing without the heart, and vice versa. The combination of the two can create Energy that is unmatched. I believe when the heart is included we can rise above that 8% and explore the true power of ourselves. Someone told me recently that Energy works like a figure eight from head to heart. Always Moving. And we all know that a figure eight is the same shape as the infinity symbol. So, I think that's reason enough for all of us to believe that in the right situations, anything is possible.

Find the wonder that makes you feel alive, and the Universe will respond in kind. It will create an Energy that is purely magical. That feeling of discovering a new world. To gasp at the beauty of something so "ordinary" we forget just how amazing it truly is. Like how a grasshopper can jump a distance that is equal to about 90 feet if compared to a human. Or how a dog's sense of smell is about 100,000 times more powerful than ours. How octopuses have three hearts and Butterflies actually smell with their feet. Or when you discover that a narwhal is actually a real freakin' animal, like a unicorn of the sea! Or... just look at a tree. Just stare at a tree. Look at how every branch grows off the other branch and how the leaves hang so perfectly. Or how sometimes a tree can create the most perfect shadows when the Sun hits it just right. Ahhhhhh, that is pure comfort.

When we are younger we are curious about everything, and I believe that curiosity helps us see the world as it truly is. Let's all question why the sky is blue, or be intrigued by how gravity is the sticky stuff that keeps us on Earth. There may never be an answer that will truly justify the curiosity, but that shouldn't diminish our fascination. Let's wonder at how the waves of the ocean are created by the moon. Let's wonder at the crazy creatures who live under the sea. How cave drawings were the Instagram of the Time. Or how we can't have comedy without tragedy. Light without dark. Let's wonder about the benefits of rain and how it's the main ingredient in all rainbows. Let's wonder how the Northern Lights are actually created. Or how serendipitous moments somehow comfort us. Or how those who passed on are still with us. How Music, or laughter, can somehow cure us. How there are moments where Time does actually slow down. Let's find the Energy we cannot see, so it can power our journey. And let's wonder in how the Sun, which doesn't do anything more than exist, can continuously affect all things in nature. Including how it can create an illusion every single day, around the world, that technically is categorized as ordinary. Yet, it has the power to transport us back to the curious mind of a child.

May the wonder be with you.

From the Wandering Mind of bernie freytag.

Find Wonder in the Ordinary Coloring Book

While reading this book did you have the desire to color some of the cartoons? Did you think you had better captions for the cartoons, too? Well, now is your chance as this coloring book will not only allow you to color many of the drawings in this book, but also create your own captions as well. Fun for ALL ages!

The Curious Reality In Our Imagination; A Creative Odyssey

An inspirational memoir chronicling Bernie's journey of discovery exploring the many mysteries within creativity, including the place (or space) where many artist's minds may travel to produce their creations...and how it may blend into a collective reality. A book filled with original prose, poetry, and illustrations conjured during this literary pilgrimage of wonder and awe.

wandering@berniefreytag.com

 /wanderingbernie   @wanderingbernie    @wanderingbernie

Made in United States
North Haven, CT
16 June 2023

37826161R00115